Welcome to the Club, Daddy

All the Secrets About Becoming a Father
(That No One is Telling You)

By Philip C. Wrzesinski

Published by Phil's Forum Publishing

   phil@philsforum.com

   3025 Warwick Road
   Jackson, MI 49201

   (517) 787-4500 phone
   (517) 787-4580 fax

Jacket Design by Joel D Canfield
Cover Image by Asia Sanchez
Interior Layout by Leigh Anne Aston
Printed by Thomson-Shore
Printed in the United States of America

ISBN 978-0-9842460-1-4

Table of Contents

Dedication:

*This book is dedicated to my wife, Shannon.
She did all the heavy lifting.*

Introduction

"It is a wise father that knows his own child." —
William Shakespeare

If you are reading this then most likely you are about to become a new dad. If you are not, did you read the cover? Go back and read the cover and determine if you want to keep reading.

Go ahead. I will wait…

Welcome back.

First, let me make it absolutely clear. I am not a doctor. I am not a nurse or any other medical professional. My medical background consists of some first aid and CPR classes and a few hours watching ER. I am not a psychologist, not a marriage counselor, not a pediatrician (nor have I played any on TV.) I am not even the Daddy Club president.

Bottom line is this. Take everything I say with a huge block of salt. Every child is different. Every birth is different. Every experience is different. At the end of the day no one in or out of the Daddy Club will know your child better than you. Not me. Not your doctors or nurses. Not your mother or mother-in-law. Just you and your wife.

What I am is a father of two wonderful boys who got to experience a couple of interesting births courtesy of my wife. And, with her permission, I am willing to share my mistakes, my triumphs and what I have learned along the way that I think every new dad should know. I am a member of the Daddy Club, a club you are about to join.

And I know the secret handshake (revealed later in the book.)

You might as well know, I also own a store that sells toys and baby products so I am in contact with expectant couples and new parents every single day. They love to share with me the joys and trials of their new families. You will, too. It is okay to brag about your kids. Just be prepared to listen to others brag about theirs.

What you are about to read in this book is the same information I have been teaching twice a month since 2003 at our local hospital. It is a class just for expectant daddies. The new dads in that class often approach me months or even years later and thank me for the practical, dad-focused advice. And sometimes the new moms approach me to thank me, too. Then they usually ask, "What did you say to get my husband so motivated for this child?"

Either way, my hope is that what you read in this book will scare you, prepare you, and excite you about the prospects of taking care of this new baby and – sometimes more importantly – taking care of your wife.

As a quick side note, in the class and in this book I will often refer to the mother of your child as your wife. Frankly, it is not my concern whether you are married or not, nor is it a reference to the sanctity of marriage or a slight at those who have not gone through the ceremony. It is simply easier that way. Deal with it.

Are you about to become a new dad? Strap it on. The road to initiation into this club is a wild ride. You drive. I'll navigate.

Section 1

Your Life is Going to Change

"I'm lucky. Sometimes I even forget I'm pregnant. And then, boom! I get a kick in the stomach!" – Heidi Klum

1. Pregnant Women Do Crazy Things

When I teach this class in person I ask every guy in the room to share the craziest thing his wife has done since she got pregnant. We get our fair share of mood swings, morning sickness and food cravings. Pickles and ice cream? Boring. How about pickles, ice cream and hot sauce?

One of my favorite stories was a guy who took his wife, on her request, to Burger King. As soon as they ordered their food she demanded they leave immediately. She was going to be sick. So they left before the food came, and went to McDonald's. Once again they ordered their food and before it arrived she had him marching back out to the car. Next stop Taco Bell. For the third time they ordered and she needed to leave. This time he

7

sent her to the car, waited for the food, and ate it before heading out to check on her.

I have heard everything from crying at a Bud Lite commercial – and, no not one of those touching ones, one of the comical ones – to leaving her car keys in the refrigerator. One guy even bragged about how his wife's farts finally stunk.

My own wife lost her sense of balance while pregnant. At five months, she was riding her bike and fell while riding over a garden hose. Her doctor told her to quit riding the bike.

Sometimes I get guys telling me their wives have done nothing crazy. So I ask them. Morning sickness? Mood swings? Nesting? (you know, that crazy cleaning frenzy where she has you on your hands and knees washing baseboards... for the third time in a week?) One guy admitted that yes, his wife had morning sickness. I had to ask, "Was she throwing up every day before she got pregnant?" That's crazy stuff.

You know what causes the craziness?

Right. Hormones. Well, more likely an imbalance or at least changing levels of hormones. Like I said, I'm not a doctor.

2. The Big Lie

How long do those hormonal changes last? How long is a pregnancy? Nine months? Forty weeks?

Yeah, that is what they have been telling us all these years. They figure if we know the end is in sight we can put up with about anything.

The truth is that it takes nine months or forty weeks (look at the calendar and count the weeks in any nine month stretch – yeah, it equals forty) for a woman to produce a baby. In that time her body must go through some amazing changes.

First, there are the hormones we talked about. The levels she needs for producing a baby are often different than her normal baseline of health. And the levels she needs for nursing that baby are often different from pregnancy. Yeah, she is a walking ball of hormonal imbalances.

Second, her body is going through some amazing physical changes. A person is growing inside of her. Her uterus turns into a womb to hold that person. In the final weeks her pelvic bones spread to make room for that little person to pop out. Her vagina stretches to accommodate that passage, too. I can tell you guys, seeing

9

a child come out of her, you instantly think, "there's no way in heck I'll be able to get back in there." Fortunately it will shrink back to normal size.

What I am getting at is the first forty weeks are filled with changes, some more wonderful than others, which help her produce your child. But the day the baby is born, she does not just wake up her normal self. Those changes have to be unchanged, and new changes are coming.

Those unchanges and new changes can take another forty weeks to complete!

The birth is not the end of the pregnancy. It is only the middle. (Those dirty, rotten liars!)

3. Physical, Emotional, and Hormonal Changes

Once the baby is born her body starts the process of changing back. Hormones are changing to meet the new needs of a nursing mom. The physical changes such as the womb shrinking back into a uterus and the pelvic bone and vagina returning to their normal shapes and positions begins. Plus, she starts growing breasts. Big, full, tender, sore, milk-machine breasts that you don't get to touch.

10

And there is another change worth mentioning… emotional change.

Think about it like this.

The day before the baby is born we call her a pregnant woman. Society has an expectation of pregnant women that they will do crazy things like have uncontrollable mood swings, bizarre food cravings, incredible urges to over-clean everything (see Chapter 1.)

The day after the baby is born she has a different name. Mom. With it comes a whole new set of expectations. Moms are caring and nurturing and always know the right thing to say or do. Yeah, a pretty unfair expectation, I know. But hey, I don't make the rules.

Yet, what really happens to her in those two days? Let's see. She gets no sleep. She is in a whole lot of pain. She pushes something out of her body that is twice the size of the opening. Hmmm…

Many women wake up the first day of motherhood and wonder when the motherhood program will get loaded into her brain. When will she instantly become caring, nurturing and always knowing the right thing to do or say? Without that, she is immediately hit with a feeling of inadequacy, like she is supposed to know but doesn't. This is a big emotional stress for many new moms.

By the way, you will have those same feelings of inadequacy that she has. But you are the guy. You are not supposed to know anything. So it is okay. You are meeting the bar of expectation. No worries.

Let us all accept the truth about your wife and the pregnancy.

The pregnancy will last well after the birth of your child because your wife will be going through **physical**, **hormonal** and **emotional** changes long after the baby arrives.

You good with that? You better be. You cannot do anything about it.

4. The Big Change for You

One of the other funny quirks of becoming a new dad is telling your friends your wife is pregnant and hearing them all respond, "Oh, your life is gonna change."

They all say that. Then they walk away chuckling, never telling you how it is going to change or what to expect during the change, or why it changes.

Until now.

The big change is this. You will become invisible. It has probably already happened. How many people have asked you recently how *you* are feeling? How many people have rubbed *your* belly? How many people have worried about how you would fare during the hot summer or the frigid winter?

You even disappear to your wife.

Women are wired for nurturing. That is how they are made. When it is just the two of you, you are the recipient of all her nurturing. You get all her attention. Sure, some of it might seem like nagging, but it is all one and the same. You are kingpin, top dog, A number 1.

But when the baby comes, you are immediately supplanted. The baby takes over the top position and rightly so. Because of the physical, hormonal and emotional changes your wife is going through, however, you do not just drop down to second. That is your wife's position. After she takes care of the baby she needs to take care of herself.

You go from number one to number three. If you have a dog, you might be number four.

Invisible. It is bad enough while she is pregnant. When the baby arrives there are now two people in the house everyone wants to see before you.

13

5. Our Role in All This

So what do we do? How do we combat this invisibility? By doing what we are wired to do.

Protect.

Who do we protect? Believe it or not, but it is not the baby. That is covered under the mom's nurturing. The person we need to protect is our wife. And more often than not, the person we need to protect her from the most is herself. She is going through physical, hormonal and emotional changes. She is not her normal health. (Note: I cannot call her sick, because that is not accurate, but she is definitely not at her baseline of health, and that is all that matters.)

When you are not your normal health what does the doctor tell you to do? Heck, what does your mom tell you to do? Get some rest. Sleep. That is exactly what your wife needs. Sleep. And more sleep. And you have to make sure she gets it.

If you do nothing else but protect her sleep you will be doing more than most new dads. You will be doing wonders for her health and your relationship. Keep that in mind as you read the rest of this book.

14

What Babies Do

"Like many other women, I could not understand why every man who changed a diaper has felt impelled, in recent years, to write a book about it."
— Barbara Ehrenreich

Babies are wonderful. They bring you lots of joy and love. At first, however, they really do not do much. They eat, sleep, cry, and go to the bathroom. Let's talk about those things.

6. Baby Wants to Eat

The best food for your baby is breast milk. There are thousands of studies, articles and books on why breast milk from momma is best for your baby, best for the mom and best for your budget. Breast milk has the best nutrients, is always the right temperature, and is readily available (as long as mom is in the room.) Breast milk helps both the baby's and the mother's immune systems. And nursing increases mom's metabolism so she loses that baby fat quicker.

For you the benefits are the money you save on bottles and formula and the fact that you do not have to get up in the middle of the night (unless you want to.)

But the medical community that is so quick to tell you how great nursing is forgets to tell you three critical things you need to know.

17

1. Breastfeeding is a learned behavior, not something babies naturally know how to do.
2. Breastfeeding takes time for babies to learn because it is the most difficult form of feeding.
3. Babies, like all humans, are generally lazy and will take the easiest path given to them.

Learned behavior. Yes it is. Don't get me wrong. Babies know they want to eat, and even know the basics of how to eat. Give them milk and they will suck it down. The key is that they are learning as they go and it takes time for them to master this new skill.

My wife found that it took three months before she and our first son fully understood the whole nursing thing. She ended up nursing him for sixteen months. So when our second son rolled around, she figured the nursing would be a breeze. Nope. Still took three months until the two of them were fully in sync.

In those first three months, while your wife is stressed with lack of sleep and the changes her body is going through, it is easy for your doctors, your parents, or others to tell you to give up the nursing and supplement with bottles and formula.

The problem with supplementing with formula is that

18

bottles and formula are far easier for babies. The milk flows easier and the baby does not have to work as hard, so babies tend to reject the breast in favor of the bottle (see rule #3 above.)

My advice? If you want the nursing to be successful, you have to protect that, too. First, by knowing that it is a learned behavior that takes about three months for mom and baby to learn, you already know there is a light at the end of the tunnel. Second, you need to find the right kind of support to get through that tunnel.

The two groups that consistently support and encourage nursing moms are the Lactation Consultants at your hospital (often called LCs) and La Leche League, a group of volunteers who typically meet monthly to help keep the art of breastfeeding alive. Seek out these groups and you will help your wife with one of the more rewarding parts of motherhood.

7. Baby Needs a Change

There are only two downsides to breastfeeding. First, breastfed babies tend to eat more often than formula-fed babies. Newborns often will nurse twelve to fifteen times a day. That is once every hour and a half to two hours.

Not much time for mom to get any decent sleep there. Second, every time they nurse, they will fill up a diaper.

Yeah, twelve to fifteen diaper changes a day. Got enough diapers yet?

Back to our earlier premise – protect your wife's sleep. One easy way to do that is to change diapers. She is expecting that you will change diapers. When you go back to work and leave her at home I can guarantee that when you get home at the end of the work day she will tell you exactly how many diapers she has changed since your last time, and how many you now owe her.

In fact, at some point down the road you will find a bunch of hash marks carved into a door jamb where she was keeping track of her diaper changes compared to yours.

The best thing for you to do is jump right in on day one and start changing diapers. Not only will you be able to give her a few more precious minutes of sleep between feedings, you will do wonders for her emotional health. She will know instantly that you are on board with this whole baby thing. You can do more for her mental health by changing the majority of the diapers than almost anything else you will do.

That said, here are some tips for making diaper changes easier.

Diaper Changing the Phil Way

Think of the diaper change as guerilla warfare. Get in. Get out. Move on.

Be Prepared

Do you go into battle unprepared? Of course not! Approach your diaper changes the same way. Prepare the area first. Get your next diaper opened to make sure both tabs are in place and the elastic is all working. Make sure you have plenty of wipes. Every diaper change starts with two wipes, some take five or six. If you need diaper rash ointments or other medicines during the change make sure they are handy, and if possible, open.

Why two wipes? Babies wear a diaper for a reason. They have no training. They spout off whenever they feel the urge. When you release them from that warm, moist diaper and the cool, dry air hits their genitals, they will release right back at you.

I raised two boys. I have to say there is some fatherly pride when you see your son pee on the ceiling. Of course, what goes up must come down so that pride is quickly replaced with, "Holy crap, look at the mess!" Invariably, some of that is going to land on you. We call that "being baptized."

Your first wipe is called the cover wipe. As soon as you open the diaper, place that wipe over the genitals. It does not stop the cannon from firing. Just minimizes the damage. Then clean that cute little bottom as quickly and efficiently as you can so you can get the next diaper on before they do too much damage.

Diaper Rashes

One of the biggest lessons I learned the hard way was diaper rashes. Our first son got a major rash on his bottom in his second week of life and it didn't clear up for forty days. Mainly because it was not a diaper rash. It was a yeast infection!

Let me back up here. Diaper rashes are common. I read a book once where the doctor described six different types of diaper rashes. There were accompanying pictures, too. Yet five of them looked exactly the same to me. And those five were treated exactly the same. Other than some funky Latin name, there was really no difference to you and me.

I tell new dads there are basically two types of diaper rashes you should know.

The first is when the bottom is pink and splotchy. Looks like a rash. Is a rash. Pretty much any diaper rash ointment will do. These rashes most often occur when the natural oils that the baby secretes in that area get blocked. And the two biggest culprits are poopy diapers and baby powder.

Yeah, baby powder. It is a drying agent, and can dry up those oils causing the baby to have a rash. Save the baby powder for its best use – removing sand from your legs and feet when you have been at the beach or sandbox. Works like a charm there and will not cause a rash.

Change those poopy diapers ASAP. I do not care if you are heading out the door to your mom's house and are already ten minutes late. Stop what you are doing and change that diaper now. Trust me, it is worth it in the long run.

The second type of rash is when you look at the baby's bottom and the whole thing is bright, screaming red. The whole area is inflamed. It looks so painful you find yourself squeezing your own butt cheeks together a

23

little harder. If you have this situation, do not think diaper rash. Think yeast infection. Then look inside the baby's mouth, at the inside of the cheeks. If you see little white bumps, this is called thrush and is another way yeast infections show their ugly face. Time to see the doctor.

You might need to get your wife checked out, too. If she is nursing, then she probably has a yeast infection, as well. If you do not get both of them on meds they will keep re-infecting each other.

Note: this is not an emergency room situation. If you notice this at 8pm at night, do not rush down to the ER. Just call the pediatrician and OB in the morning and get them checked out. The sooner, though, the better. We treated our son's yeast infection as a standard diaper rash for ten days. By then it was systemic through his body and it took us another thirty days to clear it up. During that time we thought we had a colicky baby because he cried all the time. The day it cleared, though, he became the happiest kid on the block. He was not colicky. Just had a little pain in his ass.

Jump in there and change diapers. It is not hard. And it makes a world of difference.

8. Baby is Crying

Besides eating, sleeping and pooping, babies cry. They cry a lot because that is the one true way they have to communicate with us that something is wrong. When they cry too much, we call that colic.

The definition of colic is simply "excessive crying." My only problem with that is the subjectiveness of that definition. What is excessive crying? To a sleep-deprived first-time mother with a seven day old baby it might be a minute and a half. To the mother of six, been-there-done-that it might be an hour and a half.

Chances are your baby is not colicky, crying uncontrollably for no apparent reason. If she is, know that all babies outgrow it, usually around the third month. More than likely your baby is trying to tell you something. Here are seven reasons why a baby might cry. *(Write these down and put them in your wallet. You will need this list later.)*

1. Is your baby hungry?
2. Does your baby need to be burped?
3. Does your baby need a diaper change?
4. Is your baby bothered by a diaper rash?
5. Is your baby tired?
6. Is your baby suffering from constipation/gas pain?
7. Is your baby too hot or too cold?

Is your baby hungry?

This is easy to figure out. When did she eat last? Fifteen minutes ago? That is not why she is crying. Two hours ago? That is probably why she is crying. Go feed her.

Does your baby need to be burped?

Every baby needs to burp after eating. This is the simplest thing any guy can do with a baby. Burping is simply holding a baby in an upright position until all the little gas bubbles in her belly collect into one or two big bubbles and force their way out.

Every baby has those bubbles no matter how they eat. There are bottles on the market that say on the package they eliminate gas in the baby's stomach. Liars! It is impossible. The baby breathes through her nose while eating so gas will inevitably get swallowed with the milk.

Be the Burp King in your house. As soon as your wife is done feeding, take the baby and burp her.

Two things worth noting: First, these burps are not dry. We call that spit up. If you like your shirt, put a burp cloth over it before you begin the burping process.

Second, you can pat her back, rub her back, sway a little back and forth to try to speed up the process. None of those techniques helped me, but maybe they will help you. All I knew was to wait for it. Burps are like earthquakes. There are tremors and then there is the real thing. Wait for the real thing. You will know the real thing. You will feel the real thing.

As for the spit up. Spit happens. Babies spit up a lot. But at some point I am pretty sure that your wife will question the volume of spit up coming out of your baby. She will say something like, "Look how much there is. That isn't spit up, it's throw up. We need to go to the doctor."

When she says this, do what my pediatrician told me to do. Go to the refrigerator and pull out the milk. Measure out one tablespoon of milk. Then dump that tablespoon all over the kitchen table. When you see the mess one tablespoon of milk can make you will realize that all is well with your child. It is just spit up, not throw up. Go back to bed.

Does your baby need a diaper change?

This is another easy thing to figure out. Full diapers are easy to see, feel, and smell. No real guesswork involved here. If it is dirty, change it!

Is your baby bothered by a diaper rash?

As we explained before, pink and splotchy means garden variety diaper rash. Bright screaming red means possible yeast infection. Treat accordingly.

Is your baby tired?

This is the hardest cry to decipher. So many other things can be going on. One of the first ways to crack the code is to look at the clock. What time of day? For some reason babies tend to cry in the late afternoon/early evening. They do this because their brains get full around that time.

Your baby's brain is growing at the fastest rate it will ever grow in her life. More neural pathways are being created than at any other time. That is tiring work.

You know this. If you have ever spent a day staring at a computer screen, you know how tiring brain work can be. At the end of that day you are exhausted. Yet, you did not really do anything. You did not carry shingles up a ladder to a roof. You did not dig two hundred fencepost holes. All you did was sit and stare. And you are tired.

Same thing happens with the baby. She has been awake more during the day than at night so somewhere between 4pm and 7pm she is going to announce that her brain is full for the day and she is checking out.

The way to deal with that is to think of her as being over-stimulated. To deal with this, simply remove the stimulation. Take her to a dark room. Light is a stimulation. Turn off the music. Sound is a stimulation. If you are going to have sound, make it white noise like the hum of a fan motor or static from a TV or radio. Some people say vacuuming is white noise but since that makes me cry it defeats the purpose.

Then remove the physical stimulation. You do that by swaddling your baby. Wrap her up tight in a blanket so that she feels safe and comforted.

(Don't know how to swaddle? Take my class and I'll teach you the easiest swaddling method known to man. Can't take my class? Go buy some swaddling blankets – little straitjackets for kids. They are actually easier than my folding technique – if not slightly more barbaric.)

Is your baby suffering from constipation or gas pain?

If your baby has not pooped in a while, she might start acting fussy.

Our first son did this. He pooped pretty much every

time he nursed. But sometimes he would go three or four feedings without pooping. At that point it would be impossible to get him to settle down. Our solution was simple. Since my wife was nursing, she simply altered her diet a little before the next feeding. She would eat apple sauce or yogurt or something with a lot of fiber. Without fail, the next time she nursed him, he pooped. Of course he had a lot of poop to come out by that time. And it was always my turn to change the diaper. Hmmm…

One of my favorite stories came from a buddy of mine. He was first of my friends to have kids, so we learned a lot from his trials and tribulations.

On the night in question he came home at 7:30pm to find his wife standing in the doorway holding their nine-month old son. She handed the boy over saying, "Here. He's been crying for ten minutes and I can't get him to stop. I'm tired and need to go to sleep."

My friend took his boy and did the smartest thing he could do. He took the kid into their finished basement, thus taking the crying child as far away from the sleep-deprived mom as possible. She got to go back to sleep while he dealt with the problem.

Being an engineer, this was one problem he was not

going to let go unresolved. But after three hours of trying to calm his son, my friend finally threw in the towel. Something was wrong that he could not find. He needed to take his son to the hospital.

Two steps up the basement stairs to tell momma they were going to the hospital his son looked up at him, let out a really large fart, belched equally as loud, smiled once and fell asleep. Just a little gassy, Dad.

The only thought they had was that their son ate broccoli for the first time that day. Do me a favor. When you get to the solid food stage, usually around the sixth month, introduce the foods one at a time and give each food a couple days to see if your child has any funny reactions.

One final way to deal with gas pain is to sit with your legs forming a lap. Lay your child on her back on your legs and bicycle her legs or rub her belly to alleviate gas pains. Basically, like burping, you are raising that orifice to the sky and waiting for the bubbles to break free.

Is your baby too hot or too cold?

We have a tendency to over-dress our babies. I see this all the time in my store.

Customer comes in with the baby in a onesie, pants, socks, booties, a shirt, a sweater, a jacket, a hat and a blanket thrown over the car seat… and it is the middle of July! A few minutes later the baby is crying. Mom goes to pick her up and she is soaking wet. Sweated right through her clothes.

Or in the winter she bundles up baby in a nice new snowsuit and goes to the mall to walk with her friend. Once inside she unzips the baby's snowsuit. Would you want to walk through the mall in an unzipped snowsuit? Of course not!

Or we leave them swaddled up long after they have calmed down. Swaddling is a means to an end, not the end itself. After she calms down, unwrap her before she overheats.

Babies need our help in monitoring their temperature. One of the ways we do that is in how we dress them. The rule of thumb is this. Dress the baby as you dress yourself. If it is shorts and t-shirt weather for you, it is shorts and t-shirt weather for the baby. If it is sweater and long pants weather for you, it is sweater and long pants weather for the baby.

(Disclaimer: if it is shorts and t-shirt weather for you, but

sweater and long pants weather for your wife, go with the sweater and long pants. It saves arguments in the long run.)

9. Other Techniques for Crying Babies

Crying babies are often the fingernails on a chalkboard to a sleep-deprived new mom. The more you can do to help her out, the better sleep she will get.

The checklist above is a start. But sometimes it takes more than that to calm a fussy baby. Here are some other things you can do.

Go for a walk

With your baby! Take the kid with you. Put her in a stroller, front carrier, sling, backpack or whatever is appropriate and hit the road. Where? Does not matter. Just get out of the house. This is good for four reasons.

First, by doing this you remove the crying baby from the place where momma is trying to get some sleep. That one thing alone helps your wife get the sleep she so richly deserves.

Second, the fresh air does wonders for crying babies. When our first son had his yeast infection and was crying all the time, sometimes all it took was the cool October air on the front porch to get him to settle down.

Third, babies love motion. Ever see a mom pushing a stroller who stops to talk to her friends? What does she have to do with the stroller? Yep, push it back and forth until she resumes her walk. Constant motion, baby, constant motion.

The best pacifier in the world is the car seat. The vibrations soothe even the fussiest babies. You do not get the benefits of fresh air, but your baby will be asleep before you get to the end of the block. (Of course, that does not mean you pull back in the garage. Go hit the drive-thru at least and enjoy a little free time.)

Fourth, when new dads go out in public by themselves with a baby, the hottest women in town will come up to them and finally give them the time of day, mainly because these women know the guys are safe. These guys are taken.

(Note: to any wives reading this… I made that last one up. There are only three reasons. Really, just three. Nothing to worry about.)

The Dirty Laundry Trick

One big complaint I hear is that the daddy does everything mentioned above and it never seems to work, while the baby settles instantly in momma's arms. That is because the baby does not yet know you.

This is an easy problem to solve. Simply go to the laundry basket and pull out one of your wife's dirty shirts and drape it over you the next time you go to pick up the baby. She will get the scent of mom along with the scent of you and pretty soon she will know your scent as well as your wife's.

To speed up this process have your wife do the same. Get one of your shirts from the laundry – *not the one you sweated through playing basketball at the Y* – and drape it over your wife next time she picks up the baby.

This little trick can change things dramatically in less than twenty-four hours.

The more you can do to help with the crying baby, the more sleep your wife will get. Forget the Hokey Pokey. *That* is what it's all about.

Section 3

Your Concerns

"We worry about what a child will become tomorrow, yet we forget he is someone today." — *Stacia Tauscher*

10. Dads Have Feelings Too

Just because you are invisible does not mean that your concerns are not valid. There are plenty of things guys worry about when expecting a kid. What kind of dad will I be? What if I do not know what to do at the birth? Will my baby be healthy?

The Fathers Forum published a list of the **Top Ten Concerns of Expectant Fathers**.

1. Will our baby be healthy?
2. How much pain will my wife be in?
3. What if I don't know what to do at the birth?
4. What if my wife has complications during the delivery?
5. What will it be like to be a father; what kind of dad will I be?
6. How will our relationship change after the baby?

39

7. How will having a baby affect us financially?

8. Will I be able to spend time I need to at work and also the time I want to with our baby?

9. How will my wife be as a mother?

10. How will sex change for us after the baby is born?

Copyright © Father's Forum

All rights reserved

That list is as good as any for this discussion. Let's talk about these concerns…

11. Will Our Baby Be Healthy?

The short answer is simply, "I don't know." Yeah, that sounds like a cop out answer. The truth is, we really do not know exactly how babies will turn out. We do not know if they will be healthy. We do not know if there is a hidden defect that does not show up until they drop dead on a basketball court at age nineteen.

What I do know is that whatever happens in regards to your child's health will be uniquely your own experience. You will know nothing else. In fact, that is one of the coolest things about having children. Every single experience is different. No one will have the exact same experience as you.

40

I also know that if you are blessed with a so-called "special needs" child, your life will be no more difficult than someone with a so-called "healthy" child. It will just be different. The challenges you will face will be different than the challenges someone else will face.

My cousin pointed this out to me one night around the campfire. We were camping with our boys. His son has cerebral palsy and needed assistance while growing up to do many physical tasks that you and I take for granted including walking.

He never had to worry about his boy going for a walk around the block by himself at the age of two because we said, "Let's go for a walk," but stopped just short of the door to change the newborn's diaper. Yeah, my oldest boy did that. It was scary when the neighbor behind us called to say our son was with him (and we did not even know he was missing!)

He never had to worry about his son locking the bathroom door at the new house, turning on the sink, and using the pewter bowl you got from the wedding to scoop the water out of the sink faster, ruining both the bowl and the sink, because it was not overflowing fast enough. Yeah, my boys did that. You should have heard my wife on the phone screaming about what *"your boys"* did and the four inches of water in our new basement.

Whether your child is healthy or not, the experiences you have will be your own and will be as wonderful and as challenging as you make them.

12. How Much Pain Will My Wife Be In?

Short answer? A whole hell of a lot!

The good news is that she is uniquely equipped to handle that pain. How do I know? Women have been giving birth to babies all over the world for centuries and there is still only two ways for kids to come out – front door and side door. What are there? Something like 9 billion births in the world so far? Yeah, she is equipped to handle it. Probably better than you are.

Bill Cosby has a comedy routine where he likens labor pains to pulling your bottom lip up over your head. Since you cannot do that, I figure you ought to have some frame of reference to help you understand her pain.

Have you ever hit your thumb with a hammer? What did you do? 99% of the men I know, when doing something dumb like that will say a few choice words (regardless if there are any children or women present)

and then drop or throw the hammer. My wife called that a fair assessment of the kind of pain she went through. Except she hit her proverbial thumb every two minutes for twelve hours!

The other good news you need to know about the pain your wife is in is that she will forget that pain. In fact, most of the details of the labor and the actual birth will become a blur to her. Even that really bad burning pain that happens after she pushes out the placenta. She will forget that. You will never forget the pain she was in. It will be seared across your brain. But she will forget.

You will know when she has forgotten. She will look at you and say, "Honey, let's have another kid." Yep, totally forgotten. As a warning... when that pain hits the next time around, it will be your fault for not reminding her about it.

13. What if I Don't Know What to Do at the Birth?

This is pretty easy to figure out based on the last concern. Protect her. Take care of her. Understand that she is in a whole lot of pain and cannot see or think straight.

43

When you hit your thumb with a hammer, can you thoughtfully listen to anything someone tells you at that moment? Of course not. So do not say anything to her while she is having a contraction. Do not let the nurses or doctor say anything to her then, either. She will not hear them. In other words, it is your job to be her eyes, her ears, her advocate in that room.

There is a whole profession of people called Doulas whose only job is to take care of the mom during the pregnancy. They are phenomenal people with plenty of training and experience. They can really make a difference in the stress levels of a delivering mom-to-be. But in my mind they are doing what should automatically be your job. Protect your wife.

Make sure she is comfortable. Talk to the nurses and doctors to find out what they recommend. Make sure your wife understands all instructions. Heck, make sure you do, too. If you are not clear with why she is being asked to do something, get clarification. Need ice chips? Get them. Need more towels? Get them.

For our first child one of our labor & delivery nurses was fairly inattentive. My wife's water had broken and she was leaking like a sieve. Every few minutes she felt the urge to pee. Of course, getting up meant getting a towel between her legs to keep from dripping everywhere, and it meant replacing that blue liner on the bed that kept the mattress from getting soaked. At one point we ran out of towels and liners. My wife stood by the bed for five minutes while I tried to find the nurse. Finally, I went to an unused room and emptied out the closet.

Do what you have to do to make her comfortable. Do not take anything she says personally. She just got hit with a hammer. She could not control what came out of her mouth (and she will not remember saying it anyway.) Agree with everything she says. The goal is to keep her stress down as low as possible so she can focus on not throwing that hammer at you.

14. What if My Wife Has Complications During the Delivery?

You can do everything right and still things go wrong. There are no guarantees. We ran into this with our first son.

My wife's water broke at 1:45am two days before her due date. We got to the hospital about 3:30am and got our room. They put a monitor on her to see how the labor contractions were. She told the nurse she had not felt any contractions, yet. The nurse looked at the monitor and said, "You're having one right now."

She replied, "Oh that's not bad. I can do this." *(That phrase is in the discussion for famous last words.)*

After 12 hours of Pitocin-driven labor (for you neophytes, that is the drug used to induce labor) that caused my wife serious back pain, the doctor told her the words no woman in childbirth wants to hear.

"Your baby is getting stressed and we need to get him out."

Let me backtrack for a moment. Back pain labor is the worst kind of labor. It is like hitting your thumb with a hammer while someone punches you in the kidneys. I had to push on the small of my wife's back during each contraction. To get her to breathe during these contractions I got her to sing. We sang pop songs, oldies, country & western, show tunes, patriotic songs. We even sang Christmas Carols.

It still was not enough to get our son out into the world. An emergency c-section was coming our way.

If you get so blessed with an emergency caesarean section you have to understand two things.

46

First, your wife is going to feel like a complete failure. She failed at doing the one thing that makes her better than you – having a baby. This is a normal reaction on her part and you have to give her a moment to grieve. Let her have that feeling. Do not try to suppress it.

Do not let it linger, either. Because, second, the emergency (or "unscheduled" as they call it in this politically correct world) c-section is a damn good alternative to what used to happen. In the old days, if the baby did not come out as planned, either the baby died, the wife died, or both died. Personally I will take the unplanned c-section and call it good.

You have to be prepared first for the grief, and second for the pep talk to remind her that although this is not the method you preferred, it is only a single moment in the child's life and that everything will be okay.

Maybe it won't. Let us not dwell on that quite yet because the next thing you need to do is explain that they are going to take your newborn child away in this case. The standard procedure is to immediately take the child to what is often known as the "special needs nursery." Even if the baby looks completely normal, she is being whisked away. You, as the father, as the one person not strapped to a table and under the influence of anesthesia, must go with her.

And you'd better tell your wife where you are going. In fact, before you even get to the hospital you have to go through a worst-case scenario discussion. If there is an emergency and your child gets removed from the mom, you go where the baby goes. Period. End of story. (Yeah, it is a short discussion.) You are now the advocate for that child and have to make the hard decisions about what care the child is to receive.

Also know that you probably will not see your wife for a while. As I was following our son to the special needs nursery no one gave me a clue how long it would be before my wife and I reconnected.

I was lucky. My son was just fine. I got to sit in the special needs nursery and hold him. And hold him. And hold him. Ninety minutes later I was starting to wonder why no one had come to get us. The nurse in the room had her back to me and I was too tired and shy to say anything to her. I was hoping she would look at me first, but she never did.

Fifteen minutes after that I was starting to worry. I remembered the stories about my wife's mom almost

48

dying on the operating table when her sister was born. I imagined that the whole reason the nurse was sitting with her back to me was that she knew there was bad news and did not want to be the one to tell me. She was waiting for the doctor to tell me like in all the movies and TV shows.

At the two hour mark I was about to panic. I was looking down at my newborn son thinking I had no idea how I was going to raise him by myself. I was starting to get scared when the door to the nursery opened wide. My heart sunk thinking it was the doctor with the bad news. Instead a nurse popped her head in the door and said, "Mr. Wrzesinski, your wife is ready to see you. Bring the baby and follow me."

Learn from me on this, guys. If there is a complication, first let your wife grieve the loss of not having a baby the old-fashioned way. Second, reassure her that everything will be all right. Third, you go where the baby goes. And fourth, do not panic. It always takes longer than they expect. Plan on it.

15. What Will it Be Like to Be a Father? What Kind of Dad Will I Be?

It will be awesome to be a father! As long as you become the father you want to be. That is the simple truth to this concern. You get to be the kind of father you choose. It is multiple choice with thousands of acceptable options.

Oh, sure, you will hear yourself saying the exact same things your father said to you. What is really cool is that you only have to copy the parts of your father you really liked. Then you can steal the parts of your friends' fathers that were cool to you. You can get tips from grandfathers. You can even plot out your own brand new course for fatherhood.

When I was a child we used to take trips up to Grayling, Michigan and stay on the Manistee River. There was a putt-putt golf course with a big elephant and hippo in it along the way to the river. I always wanted to play putt-putt golf. I love to play putt-putt golf. But my parents, serious golfers that they are, never liked to stoop to that level of golf. We only played there once in the ten years I remember driving by.

Now I am the parent. When I want to play putt-putt,

we play putt-putt. I get to choose.

All that really matters as a father is that you do three things well.

First, love your wife as best you can. You are the role model your kids will follow for what a healthy relationship should look like. My grandfather says the best way to be a great dad is to be a great husband. I agree.

Second, love your kids as best you can. Even when they make mistakes. Even when they cause you embarrassment. Love them for who they are, not who they might become.

Third, let them make mistakes. Mistakes are the best teachers. Let them make mistakes and learn from them. You are going to make mistakes as a parent. Make sure you learn from your mistakes and help them learn from theirs.

You get to be the father you want to be. Be that father and be it proudly.

16. How Will Our Relationship Change After the Baby?

That is pretty much what this whole book is about.

The two main factors to remember are:

First, you are no longer number one in the household. The baby is top dog, king pin, number one recipient of your wife's nurturing.

Second, you can move right back up the scale to a close second place if you take care of your wife through the post-birth part of her pregnancy by protecting her sleep and showing her support and love.

If you remember those two things your relationship will most likely get even stronger.

17. How Will Having a Baby Affect Us Financially?

There are three main expenses involved with having a baby:

1. Baby Products
2. Diapers/Formula
3. Health Care Costs

Yeah, diapers and formula could be considered baby products but since they are consumables and a huge expense, I have separated them out for this discussion.

Baby Products

I have a lot of knowledge here. I have been selling

baby products for the better part of two decades. There is a lot of money to be saved here.

Sure, there are a few basics you will need. A crib and mattress, clothing, a car seat if you drive anywhere, a stroller or carrier if you walk anywhere, a few blankets, and plenty of burp cloths (cloth diapers work best for this.)

And there are a lot of things you do not need. If you actually stop and think about it, there are only two products specifically for the baby – the car seat and the crib mattress. Everything else is for you. Most of the products you see in baby stores today did not exist when you were born. You turned out okay.

Put your money into a top-quality car seat and a top-quality mattress. Do not simply trust the Internet ratings or even reviews from your friends. They often have not seen the latest greatest products and do not have the insider information your local baby store will have. Buy them from a local independent with a stellar reputation for integrity. He or she will be able to explain why the recommended product is the best for you.

For everything else, however, understand that these products are completely dependent on your lifestyle, your tastes and your budget. Sure, safety is a primary concern. So is knowing exactly why you need each product. Do not buy anything you do not know for certain that you need.

Diapers and Formula

Diapers and Formula are huge expenses. With formula, not only are you buying the powder, you also have to buy the bottles, and there is the added energy cost of warming the milk and cleaning the bottles. Tell your wife that the budget only allows for breastfeeding. Then get her all the support she needs to make it successful (see Section 2, Chapter 6.)

To save money on diapers, consider going with cloth. You can get through an entire child's upbringing for less than $500. Some new parents have done it for under $200. And it is a lot easier than it was when you were a child. Velcro and snaps have replaced pins. Biodegradable, flushable liners have replaced hours scrubbing off poop in the toilet.

Health Care Costs

Finally, you need to be aware of the huge medical costs associated with having a baby. You have the trip to the hospital to have the baby. Then you have the visits to the pediatrician on Day One, One Week, Two Weeks, Four Weeks, Three Months, Six Months, and One Year. Those are just the "well visits." Throw on top of that about five or six unplanned visits when your child is running a huge fever or has a funny cough or that dreaded yeast infection.

If you have insurance and your child will be covered under that policy, I recommend you go talk to the administrator of that plan today and see what hoops, if any, you will have to jump through.

For instance, here in Michigan, Blue Cross Blue Shield requires that the kid have his own social security number before he will be covered. That is good information to know. Our local hospital actually gives you the form to fill out for a social security number right after you have the baby. Fill it out. Give it to the nurse. A few hours later he has a number. Now his identity can be stolen, but at least he is covered by BCBS.

I had a friend who did not jump through this hoop and subsequently a few hospital bills regarding the baby did not get paid. For whatever reason, he never saw those bills. A year later he went to buy a car and his credit score had taken a huge hit from those unpaid bills.

Find out what you need to do to get your child covered. If you do not have insurance, see if there is some agency in the county that can help you decipher all the state programs available to you. My local health department offers that service in our area.

18. Will I Be Able to Spend Time I Need to at Work and Also the Time I Want to With Our Baby?

Of course you will. How? I do not know. You will figure it out.

I often look back on my pre-child life and wonder what I did with all my spare time. I still play golf. I still play my guitar. I still work a second job on top of my main job running a retail store. I still have time to exercise and go out on dates with my wife.

And I spend plenty of time with my boys.

For me, the thing that changed my priorities was love. You may have heard someone say that you do not know love until you have a child. There is some truth to that statement. The love you will feel when you look at your newborn baby has a power that you have not yet felt. The hard part is trying to explain it to someone who has not yet felt it.

The best way I have found is to put it into a perspective you might understand – sports. Having a baby is more powerful than winning the Super Bowl. Having a baby is more wonderful than winning the Daytona 500. Having a baby is more life-altering than getting elected to the baseball Hall of Fame.

How do I know? The guys that have done both have told us. You have heard it. Guy wins the Super Bowl and what does he say? "Other than the day my child was born, this is the greatest day of my life." Goose Gossage said this in a radio interview when he got elected to the Hall of Fame, "Other than the two days my children were born, this is the greatest day of my life."

Heck, Sylvester Stallone wrote it in the screenplay of Rocky II!

The day your child is born will instantly take over the top spot in your heart for greatest day of your life all because of love. Your priorities in life will change. You will do whatever is necessary to make sure you can do your job to provide for your family and spend the time you want with your child. Trust me. It just works out that way.

19. How Will My Wife Be as a Mother?

This is a little bit trickier. Sure, you can look at the mother figures in her life to see the role models she has from which to draw her style of parenting. Like you, she gets to choose what kind of mom she wants to be.

In fact, I suggest the two of you start talking now about parenting styles. You are free to alter your style at any time as you get more comfortable with your roles and new information presents itself, but the earlier you start talking about the kind of parents you want to be, the better your chances of succeeding at that.

One thing to keep in mind… She will have a tougher time being an awesome mother if she is sleep-deprived and stressed out. See what you can do to help her with that.

20. How Will Sex Change for Us After the Baby is Born?

Finally, the question you all wanted answered and were afraid to ask. Be honest, did you skip to this question first?

The best way to answer that question is to rephrase it. How long do you have to wait before you have sex again?

58

The doctor might tell you six to eight weeks. Maybe a little bit longer if she had any complications like a c-section, a torn perineum, or a broken tailbone. Remember, she is not her normal health at this moment. You wouldn't jump in the sack if she had bronchitis, would you? There is already a short window of waiting that is required.

What I like to tell guys, however, is that if you do not do what we have been talking about, if you do not protect her sleep and support her through this period, you are going to wait a heck of a lot longer.

Physically, she will change back to her normal size and be quite capable of a healthy, happy sex life. The key for you is to help her change back to normal emotionally. You do that by being involved in the child-rearing and protecting her sleep to get her back to normal as quickly as possible.

There are other benefits. Most of you reading this book have a wife under the age of thirty. When do women hit their sexual peak? In their thirties. And it is not a peak. It is more of a plateau. Thirty five to forty is the generally accepted time period of her sexual peak (although all women are different, but you already knew that.)

Would you like to be in the game when she hits that peak? Of course you would! Take good care of her. It pays off big in the long run.

What Every Guy Should Know

"The only source of knowledge is experience." —
Albert Einstein

21. Resources

In my class I use a lot of information from other resources to frame the conversation. Then I give my opinion on the topic including why I agree or disagree and what more you should know.

One of my favorite resources comes from a website that was originally www.NewDads.com but now can be found at www.DadsAdventure.com. They had a ***Top Ten Things Every Dad Should Know*** list that is one of the key elements in my class. The list does not exist there anymore, but the information from the site is still spot-on.

There are literally dozens of books for new dads on the market, too. I am sure there are bloggers out there telling you everything you need to know one post at a time. Maybe you will have the inspiration to blog about your own experience. Even if no one reads it, you will have an awesome record of your new life with your child.

The most important point here is to know that not every dad out there will just laugh at you and walk away when you tell them your wife is expecting. There are plenty of us who want to help, who want your experience to be every bit as wonderful as ours.

You just need to do a little digging.

22. Top Ten Things Every Dad Should Know

Here is the list from NewDads I use, exactly how it looks when I pass it out.

1. Trust your instincts. A little experience will quickly turn you into the world's leading expert on your own baby.

2. Learn from the best. Ask the hospital nursery personnel to show you how to change, swaddle and bathe your baby. Ask other dads for suggestions.

3. When it comes to mom, remember to be patient and positive. Communication and support is the key. She'll love you for it.

4. Stand your ground. Let no one push you away

from your baby. Not your mother-in-law, your mate, your boss, no one.

5. ~~Learn as a family, just the three of you. Keep "help" in the first weeks down to what is needed lest it becomes interference.~~

6. Your baby is portable. You can take your baby anywhere. Don't get caught up in fretting about what you can't do.

7. You will get frustrated. Step back. Think. Count to some high number. Think again, and so forth.

8. Make eye contact. Babies talk with their eyes. You will see!

9. Relax and enjoy the ride. Make it a daily habit to play with your new baby, check out her tiny little feet, have him fall asleep on your chest, etc. It's the little things that count the most.

10. When times are trying, remember they too will pass. Before you know it, you will have a teenager on your hands.

As you can see, I do not think very highly of #5. That is okay. I have some different thoughts on that subject. Here are my thoughts on all ten.

23. Trust Your Instincts

Do you know why there are no owners' manuals for babies? Because every single one is different. Every single child is completely different and will require different knowledge and understanding to raise her. Only those who work with that child every day will truly know her. That would be you and your wife.

When my wife and I first announced she was pregnant we got in the mail a pull-out section from the LA Times on having a baby. Inside this tabloid was a table with six of the leading national pediatricians down the left and six topics of child-rearing across the top. Thirty-six squares in this table with the leading thoughts of the most respected names in pediatrics, and no two of them were alike! These six doctors could not agree on any single topic. In fact, no two doctors could agree on any single topic. They all had a different opinion.

What does that tell you? That there are many right ways to raise your child. You have to find the way that works best for you and trust your instincts to do it right.

24. Learn From the Best

I think the best job for a nurse in the hospital must be the post-natal wing. You typically find some of the most incredible nurses there. They love to be part of this moment in your life. They also have a wealth of knowledge they can share with you such as how to swaddle your baby, why he has that funny yellow stuff on his scalp, or what to use to clean up the meconium stool.

The way I see it, you have already paid for the room, so you might as well get your money's worth by asking questions. Knowledge is power and the more you get, the better your decisions will be.

25. Be Patient and Positive – Communication is the Key

Oh yes it is! Communication can be tricky because we have different perspectives of the matter at hand and we make assumptions based on our perspectives. Here is an example.

If you are going back to work and leaving your wife at home with the baby, understand that she is waiting for the moment you come home to turn over the parenting duties. I mean the exact moment you walk through the door. She has been timing you to know when you will be home. Has it timed to the very second so that she can shove the baby into your arms as you walk through the door and say, "Here!"

The only problem with that is if you are like me and most other guys, the moment you walk through the door you are not ready to put on that daddy hat. You need a little decompression time. You need time to change out of your work clothes, to wash your hands and face, maybe even to sit on the toilet because you refuse to sit on the toilet at work.

I had a guy in class one time who drove a garbage truck all day. He said he needed to take a shower immediately when he got home. I understand that.

Whatever it may be, you need a few moments to get into the right frame of mind. That is where the disconnect happens.

See if you can picture this conversation happening in your household…

You walk through the door and she thrusts the baby towards you saying, "Here!"

You say, "No."

You all know what is happening next. She is going off

on you. "I've been home all day dealing with this crying baby and I've had to change eight diapers and feed him eight times and your mom called twice during my naps and I haven't had a break and…"

Yeah, she will go off on you long enough for you to change your clothes, wash your hands and face, and get ready to take over. You turn to her and say, "Okay, I'll take him."

Then it happens… The hands go on the hips, the finger starts to waggle. She looks at you with that face – you know the face I mean – and says, "You're only doing this 'cause I said so. You're not supporting me."

Can you picture that conversation happening? In my class I have yet to meet a dad who could not imagine that conversation happening in his house. In fact, that conversation is happening all over America tonight. And it does not have to happen at all!

All you have to do is have a little talk with your wife before you go back to work. Tell her, "Honey, I am going back to work and I know you will be here all alone with the baby. I want to help out as soon as I get home. All I ask is that you give me five minute (or whatever you can negotiate) to get in the right frame of mind. Will you do that for me honey?"

69

Of course she is going to say yes and you avoid that nasty misunderstanding. That is what I am talking about when I say communicate.

26. Stand Your Ground!

One of the things most guys dread is the mother or mother-in-law coming to help out. The more womenfolk in the room, the more our roles get diminished.

Heck, we are already diminished. How many times have you heard a woman say, "Oh, my husband is home babysitting the kids." Bull! You are not a babysitter. You are the parent. You are home parenting. The babysitter is the fourteen year old kid down the block who took the babysitting class at Red Cross.

If you do not think that statement is demeaning, try reversing it. Try telling someone your wife is home babysitting the kids. I will be surprised if you will be able to cross your legs for a week.

With all that said, however, having a mother or mother-in-law coming in to help out is a blessing in disguise. Think about it like this. The perfect world for your wife is to eat, sleep, and feed the baby. That is it. Only three things for her to do.

Eat.

Sleep.

Feed the baby.

Everything else is now your responsibility. If you do not know how to do laundry, now is the time to learn or find someone else to do it for you. If you do not know how to clean the house, now is the time to learn or find someone else to do it for you. If you do not know how to cook, now is the time to learn or make a list of all the places that deliver so you are not stuck eating pizza every night.

And what do mothers and mother-in-laws know how to do? You got it. Cooking, cleaning and laundry. You just solved all your problems at once.

Here is what you do. When she arrives, sit her down and tell her, "I am so glad you are here. Here is OUR plan. WE need to make sure my wife (your daughter) does not have to do anything more than eat, sleep, and feed the baby. We need to protect her sleep and make sure she gets all the rest she can…"

Basically, it is like winding her up and letting her go. Plus, she will be so impressed with you for being so proactive that she will never keep you from your kid.

27. ~~Just the Three of You~~ – NOT!

This is the only part of the top ten with which I disagree. Some doctors will tell you that the first week should be just the three of you, that you need that time to bond. Do not listen to them. You have your whole life to bond. That first week will not make or break your relationship with your child.

Here is proof.

My grandfather served on the USS Arkansas Battleship during World War II. He was training for D-Day when my Mom was born. In fact, he missed the port that had the letter saying they had a girl and her name was Sue. All the subsequent letters said, "The baby did this, the baby did that." He did not even know for months what he had!

He came home long enough to meet his daughter and produce a son. That child was born while he was adrift on a powerless boat somewhere in the Pacific. He finally saw his son for the first time six weeks after he was born and just as the war ended.

As I write this my grandfather is ninety-three. Every day his son stops by and has breakfast with him. Every Sunday he has dinner with my Mom and she takes him to his bridge games and assorted lunches throughout the week. I think they are pretty well bonded.

You do not need that time to bond, you need that time to rest. You need to get as much help as possible to make sure your wife gets all the sleep she can get.

They say it takes a village to raise a child. I say employ the village on day one. If someone says, "Can I help?" say "Yes!" and give them something to do. Hand them $50 and a grocery list. Not only will they get everything on the list, they will even bring back your change.

Can I help?

Yes, can you help me sort some laundry? Yes, I haven't had a chance to mow the lawn. Yes, I need someone to pick up a prescription from the pharmacy. Yes, can you drop these thank you cards at the mailbox?

I think too many new parents get so worried about the bonding issue that they martyr themselves for the sake of bonding. Do not make that mistake. You have your whole life for bonding. Get some help.

28. Your Baby is Portable

Yes she is. Get out of the house and go do things with her. Take her to the park, to the store, to the ballgame (bring earplugs for her.) First, it is a whole lot easier to travel with a newborn than a toddler. Second, the more exposure to the real world she gets, the stronger she will be.

There is an old wives tale that says you should not leave the house for the first thirty days. Do not listen. Getting out of the house is great for babies. Fresh air is great for babies. Exposure to other people you know and trust is great for babies. Getting out of the house is great for mom, too.

My cousin is a big Detroit Tigers baseball fan. Her first child did not keep her out of the ballpark. She and her husband bought noise-reduction headphones for their daughter and enjoyed the game. Heck, it is easier to take a newborn than a toddler. The toddler requires her own ticket.

29. You Will Get Frustrated

This is a given. It happens to all of us. Because there is no owners' manual you will not always know what to do. Even if you had a book that covered all possible scenarios, by the time you referenced the right scenario and learned what to do, your kid would be in college.

One of the biggest frustrations is the crying baby. Although I have given you plenty of tips earlier in this book for dealing with a crying baby, there will come a time when you will feel so frustrated you just want to shake your baby. I know that feeling. Like every other dad on the planet, I had that feeling.

Having that feeling is normal. Acting on it is not. Shaking a baby is deadly. Do not do it! Instead, lay the baby softly down in the crib and walk away. Go outside for a couple minutes and calm yourself down. When you return you will probably find the baby still crying in the crib, but she was safe while you were away and now you are in a better frame of mind to deal with her.

Some people will tell you how important it is to pick up a crying baby, how if you do not, you will scar that child for life. They are probably right. That does not change my advice. You are going to scar your kids for life so many times, that one moment will not be enough to get them on a talk show about bad parents.

Better to scar them for life than end their lives. You have my permission to lay them down and walk away for a couple minutes.

By the way, do not feel bad for having those feelings

of frustration. We have all been there. The most important thing in those moments is doing the right thing.

Note: sometimes guys in my class will ask me if it is okay to simply let a baby cry. My answer to that is only if you do not know what to do. Babies cry to tell you something. It is your job as the parent to figure out what they are trying to say. Figure that out first, then you can decide how to respond.

30. Make Eye Contact

Babies do talk with their eyes, just not at first. Mostly they talk by crying. But they will begin to recognize you and that becomes a beautiful thing. When they see you and smile, that smile lights up the room and melts away all the troubles of your day.

My wife and I used to do a one-hour radio show for parents. We only got one negative review in our three years on the air. It was a gal who called to complain when my wife said that newborns are basically little lumps.

But really, they are. For the first couple months they do not move much. They do not communicate except when something is wrong. They make funny noises, funny smells, and big messes.

Then their eyes open to the world around them and all those noises, smells and messes fade away. That moment will happen with your child. You just have to wait for it. By the way, when I say fade away, I mean metaphorically. Those noises, smells and messes will still be there. They just will not seem as bad.

31. Relax and Enjoy the Ride

My favorite "hold" is when my son would fall asleep on my chest while I sat on the couch or comfy chair with the TV remote in hand. Feeling him breathing against my chest is one of the best feelings in the world. Plus, he is going to sleep for about an hour or so which means I have time to catch up on a little sports.

The only downside to this position is that at some point your wife will walk by and want to take the child. Do not let her. Tell her everything is fine, leave you two alone. Because if she picks up the baby, do you know what you have to do? Laundry!

32. These Times Will Pass

Do me a favor. Write it down. Write yourself notes when they do cute things. Write yourself notes when they do amazing things. Write yourself notes about how they make you feel. When they begin to talk, write down the funny things they say. You are going to forget them quickly, so write them down and date them.

Sure it seems like a touchy-feely thing to do but those notes serve three purposes. First, when the next stage in life comes, you have something to either remind you how wonderful the previous stage was, or give you tips to get through this new stage. Second, if you ever need a good laugh, go back and read some of your old notes, the older the better. You will be amazed how much *you* have grown up, too. Third, at some point you need material to embarrass your child in front of a future boyfriend or girlfriend. These notes work wonders!

The days go slow, but the years go fast. Enjoy each and every moment you can.

Section 5

Summary

"A good laugh and a long sleep are the two best cures." – Old Irish Saying

33. Use This Advice

I mentioned earlier that my wife and I used to host a one hour radio show for parents. We started the show after our first child was born but before the second. Shortly after that we launched a website with information from the show.

After son number two arrived, we posted our tips for new parents. All the things people told us to do before number one son arrived, but we did not do until number two arrived, and then kicked ourselves for not doing it the first time.

The best advice I can give you? Use the advice you get!

Most of it is pretty good. Some of it is way out there. The best way to figure out which is which is to try it all. You and your wife are smart enough to recognize when it

81

is not working out.

The next few chapters are the last few chapters. Think of them as a review of everything previously discussed with a few new thoughts thrown in to keep you interested. If you do nothing else with this book, memorize these chapters and use this advice. Period.

34. Accept Help

This is not the time to be martyr. This is not the time to prove to the world how much you can do on little sleep. This is not the time to hunker down and become isolated from the world.

If someone says, "Can I help?" Say "YES!"

There is more to do than time to do it so get your friends, your family, your neighbors, your co-workers involved. Make a list of all the things that need to be done and keep it handy. As soon as someone offers assistance, pull out the list and give that person an assignment.

Don't be shy about it. Get ALL the help you can get. You can pay them back when they have a kid.

35. Sleep When the Baby Sleeps

I am talking about your wife, not you. She is the one going through the physical, hormonal, and emotional changes. She is the one who has to offer up her nipples to the baby every two hours or so. She needs the sleep. Make sure she gets it.

The symptoms of Sleep Deprivation include things like Anxiety, Fatigue, Depression, Lack of Hygiene, Anti-Social Behavior, Hormonal Imbalances (like she really needs more of that.)

The symptoms of Postpartum Depression (PPD) are almost identical.

Yet for some reason, when I searched Wikipedia there was not one single mention of lack of sleep being a potential cause for postpartum depression. Not one!

Someone is asleep at the wheel.

Look at what sleep deprivation causes... Depression, confusion, headaches, irritability, hormonal imbalances, ADHD and psychosis. You do not need a fancy degree to see that lack of sleep and PPD have to have some sort of connection.

Even if the doctors are right and sleep-deprivation does not lead to PPD, what I can tell you that you already know is that sleep is the greatest tool for getting someone back to normal health. Ever!

If you protect your wife's sleep, she will feel better both physically and emotionally. That is undisputed. If she feels better physically and emotionally, then you have lessened the chance of her falling into postpartum depression.

PPD is real. It is scary. We do not conclusively know what causes it. I know that my wife suffered from it to the point of needing medication. And I know I did not do the kind of job I should have done to protect her sleep.

I am going with what I have observed with my own eyes. Protect your wife's sleep and she will be better for it. You will, too. Her memory of things like that is pretty good. Your reward is coming later.

36. Have Your Friends Cook for You

You are busy enough. The easiest way to get your friends involved is to schedule seven of them to cook dinner for the two of you every other night for the first two weeks you are home.

Pick the seven best friends that know how to cook (or give them the phone number for Outback takeaway)

and write up a schedule. Stack the order from worst to best. That first night you will be so tired that anything will taste good.

Why every other night? Because it is difficult to cook for two. There will be leftovers tonight. Eat those tomorrow night and prepare for something new the next night.

Post the list so that everyone on the list knows who is cooking when. That way you get the phone call...

"Phil, this is Cheryl. What did Shelley bring last night?"

You know that whatever Shelley brought, Cheryl wants to top it. That's how those ladies work. Make it, and them, work to your advantage.

37. Keep Daddy Involved

Yeah, that is pretty much what this whole book is about. But here are some other things for you to do.

Pack the Diaper Bags

Yes, I said "bags", plural. Pack more than one. If she got more than one at the shower, keep the extra ones. If she wants to return one, tell her you will do it and then throw it in your trunk till after the baby is born. She will never know the difference.

If you are going back to work and leaving her home alone, it is your duty to make sure she can get out of the house whenever possible. One simple way to do that is to pack a couple diaper bags every night before you go to sleep. Make it part of your nightly routine. Brush your teeth, go to the bathroom, wash your hands and face, pack the diaper bag, go to sleep.

That way, when she wants to leave the house she does not have to think twice about the diaper bag being ready. She can even leave the house twice in one day without thinking about it! You will win more brownie points for this one act than you deserve.

What goes in a diaper bag? Diapers, lots of them. In fact, the rule of thumb is that if you have room in your diaper bag you do not have enough diapers packed.

My worst diaper change ever happened at my parent's house. I pulled out the changing pad from the diaper bag and prepared to change number one son's five-wiper blowout poopy diaper. Of course those changes also require an outfit change so I pulled a new diaper and a clean onesie from the diaper bag and started in on the cleanup.

Remember this was before I knew about the cover wipe. The trouble, however, began when I went to put on the new diaper and accidentally ripped off one of the Velcro tabs (diaper #1.) When I went back to the diaper bag for a new diaper my son immediately peed all over everything. The new outfit (outfit #1), the changing pad, me, and oh yes, the new diaper (diaper #2) all got soaked.

I cleaned up that mess, got out another diaper (#3) and slid it under his bottom, at which point he immediately pooped all over it. In frustration I yanked out the diaper only to watch helplessly as the poop launched from that diaper onto the next clean outfit (outfit #2.)

One more round of cleanup and one more round of onesies (#3) and diapers (#4), I finally had him covered up. I swear to you, however, that the moment I finished that diaper change he was filling the front of his diaper one more time. I handed him to my wife and said, "Your turn."

One diaper change. Four diapers. Three outfits. Endless number of wipes. And a mother laughing in the background. It could happen to you.

Make sure you have plenty of diapers, wipes, outfits and a clean changing pad. One more thing to add to your diaper bag packing list is Ziploc bags. Quart-sized, freezer style preferred. These are for keeping those dirty outfits separate from the clean contents of your diaper bag until you get home to do laundry. Shove about six or eight of those into the diaper bag, too.

Prepare Some Snacks

Another simple thing to do is to put together some simple snacks for your wife in little baggies. Crackers & cheese, sliced fruit, apples & peanut butter, etc. If all she is supposed to do is eat, sleep, and feed the baby, she does not have a lot of time for food prep. Do it for her if you can. It makes a world of difference.

Write Thank You Notes

You got all that free stuff. Send those people thank you notes. Even if you were not invited to the shower *(heck, you should write a note just to thank them for not inviting you)* you can still write the note or at least address all the envelopes. You are going to use most of the stuff your wife got, too.

Make it a habit to do those little things she would

normally do. It will make a difference for her, which will make a difference for you.

38. Find Her a Support Group

If you are going back to work and leaving her home alone with the child you need to help her find some adult interaction each day or at least each week. Search out mothers clubs like MOPS (Mothers of Preschoolers.) Check the classifieds, check online, check your local churches. There are groups out there. If you cannot find one, start one. Contact all those new parents in your birthing class. Talk to your friends that have babies and toddlers. Just find something for her to do.

She needs some event to which she can look forward to attending each week. It not only gives her a little reality break, it helps her own sanity. If she is home all day alone with the child talking baby talk, she will gradually go insane and take you with her.

Even if you have to bribe a friend or two to visit her daily, that little bit of adult interaction goes a long way.

39. Things Will Not Go as Planned

Finally, remember that you are no longer in charge of your life. The arc you had imagined for your life has been shifted and that tiny little bundle of joy now holds all the controls. That is okay. Run with it. Embrace the chaos and disorder. Do not worry that you are still in your pajamas at noon that first week when company arrives. Do not stress about the pile of laundry waiting to be sorted when grandma and grandpa visit. Do not drive yourself crazy trying to get everywhere on time.

Slow down and enjoy these moments. Live in the present and make the most of every memory you can. It is the chaos, not the order, which you will remember most fondly.

Postlude

Thanks for sticking it out till the end. That shows me you have what it takes to be a fantastic father and husband.

My grandfather has always said that the best way to be a great daddy is to be a great husband. You are the role model for treating spouses that your kids will remember all their lives.

I wrote this book to make a difference. I did my part. Now it is your turn.

Tonight, or whenever you see your wife next, do me a favor. Wrap your arms around her. Hold her tight. Give her a kiss on the neck right below the ear and whisper into that ear, "Honey, things are going to be great. I've got it all under control."

91

The Secret Handshake

Time for you to learn the secret handshake.

The next time you meet a guy about to have a baby do this.

- Look him straight in the eye.
- Grab his hand firmly.
- Smile.
- Shake your head from side to side.
- Tell him, "Your life is going to change."

But before you laugh and walk away, give him this book. He needs it, too. Better yet, go buy him his own copy.

Then you can laugh all you want.

Welcome to the club!

About the Author

When not playing daddy, Phil is a top-level retailer who owns and operates Toy House and Baby Too, one of the 25 Best Independent Stores in America (in the book *Retail Superstars*) and a business consultant who speaks to audiences all over the country. His passion is for helping others, whether installing a car seat, teaching parents about toys, or helping other independent retailers achieve their success.

Phil has written two books for businesses, *Hiring and the Potter's Wheel: Turning Your Staff Into a Work of Art* and *Financials Made Understandable: The Building Blocks of a Successful Toy Store*. You can learn more about Phil at www.PhilsForum.com.

Acknowledgments

This book would not exist if the Stork Club at Allegiance Health (formerly Foote Hospital) had not thought it was a good idea to have a non-medically trained daddy teach guys how to change diapers. Thank you to Barb Mierzwa and Jenny Wren and all the instructors of the Stork Club for allowing me the opportunity to talk to the guys. You have made my favorite two hours of the month possible.

Thank you to all the dads who have given me two hours of your time. There is nothing better than hearing from you how the class made a difference for you, your wife and your child.

Thank you to Joel D and Sue Canfield for thinking this book needed an audience, for editing, formatting, and designing the book and cover, and for being a wonderful partner in this project. Your help has been greatly appreciated.

Thank you to Thomson-Shore for once again printing a professional book. You make printing a book so easy.

Most importantly, a huge thank you to my wife, Shannon, the mother of our two wonderful boys. You know what you did in all this – pretty much everything. Without you, well, there would be no book. Period. Thanks for letting me share our stories and my mistakes with the world.